God's Touch

INSPIRATIONAL PRAISES, SONGS & PRAYERS

Delphine A. Brooks

Copyright © 2020, Delphine A. Brooks
God's Touch: Inspirational Praises, Songs & Prayers

Contact the Author via e-mail at
dbrenewing.hope@gmail.com

All rights reserved. No part of this workbook may be reproduced, stored in a retrieved system, or transmitted in any form or any means, electronic, mechanical, photocopying, recording, scanning, or otherwise, without the prior written permission of the author.

Author: Delphine A. Brooks
Publication Services: Kingdom News Publication Services, LLC.

DISCLAIMER

All the material contained in this book is provided for educational and informational purposes only. No responsibility can be taken for any results or outcomes resulting from the use of this material.

While every attempt has been made to provide information that is both accurate and effective, the author does not assume any responsibility for the accuracy or use/misuse of this information.

Printed in the United States of America.
ISBN 978-0998026299

All rights reserved.

KINGDOM NEWS TODAY
Publication Services, LLC

Acknowledgements

I want to truly give God the praise that is due to His name for allowing me to be touched by Him in the following works. It is from His touch that I have been so inspired to write. The faith granted unto me from Him has given me strength to endure.

To those whose inspiration is known and not known, I say thank you.

Dedication

I dedicate this book of poetry in loving memory of Shirley Brooks-Walker, my mother, through whose womb God blessed me to be conceived.

I would like to dedicate this book to my five children, grandchildren present and those to come.

I would also like to send dedication to my siblings, family and friends.

My church family has been my support and inspiration. Thanks for believing in me.

Table of Contents

Longing of Praise 1
God Is 3
All I Know 4
No More Death in the Pot 5
To Give 6
Deliverance 7
Enamored 8
Faith 9
Strengths of Faith 10
Grace 11
He Is Everything 12
His Goodness 13
Hope Eternal 14
Prayer of Confession 15
Jesus Knockin' 16
More Than a Conqueror 17
Obedience 18
Perfection 19
Holiness 20
Righteous 21
Praise Your Way Through 22
Surrender 23
The Hunter 24
Observe 25
Eternal Light 26
Gates to Our Soul 28

Be Careful	29
Life	31
The Savior's Call	32
Let the Words of My Mouth	33
A Meditation of Prayer	34
The Seed of the Woman	36
Black and White	38
A Pebble	39
Be the One	40
Desperately Aware	41
In the Process of Time	44
Is it hard?	45
Love Announces Itself	47
Life	48
Your Presence	49
Women of Excellence	50
PLEA	52
The Flower of Life	54
"My Prayer"	55
On One Note: The Horrors of Society	57
My Enemy	59
The Awesomeness of God	60
Women of God	62

AN ARRAY OF BEAUTY
Love – FRIENDSHIP – SYMPATHY – PASSION
APPRECIATION – ROYALTY - MAJESTY BEAUTY

Longing of Praise

I long to praise You and all that is within me
I long to praise Your Name
My heart beats praise
My mind thinks praise
My soul feels praise
My lips sing praise
My ears hear praise
My feet dance praise
I long to praise Your Name.

I love to praise You and all that is within me;
I love to praise Your Name.
Rocks need not cry out for me
For I WILL cry out
Trees need not bow for me
For I WILL bow
Waves need not clap for me
For I WILL clap
Let me not forget to praise thee
I long to praise You and all that is within me;
I long to praise Your Name.

I feel the pulse of praise
I feel the flow of praise
I hear the sound of praise
Coursing through the tears
Even through my fears
Coursing through my sorrow
With hope of joy for tomorrow
I long to praise You and all that is within me;
I long to praise Your Name.

God Is...

. . . my air flowing in; flowing out of my nostrils.

I breathe His goodness inside of me.

His goodness overshadows everything within.

No matter where I go; which way I turn; my air is there.

His goodness, it overwhelms me.

I submerge myself; I envelope my thoughts all in Him.

Every day is a new year.

I breathe out the old; I breathe in the new.

All I know...

Is
What's right
What's holy,
    pure
     true

Al I know
Is you

Don't know
What's best for me

All I know
    is you are the one,
      The only one
To see me through

All I know is you.

No More Death in the Pot

Where death is in the pot
The Word must be applied
To receive life
And that everlasting

Now there is purging
And sin is taken away
No more death in the pot
When Jesus comes to reside

As meal is used in making bread
Jesus is that Bread of Life, and
When the Bread is applied
No more death in the pot

Faith sees what cannot be seen
And experiences hope

Feed upon the pot of life
That you may live

Feed upon the Bread of Life
To receive life everlasting
There is no more death in the pot
Because Jesus is that Bread of Life

To Give

To give
 is to drink when you're thirsty
To feed
 is to eat when you're hungry
To share
 is to cloak you with His goodness
To provide
 is to be filled with His love

The longing of your soul can be satisfied

When you feed the least of these little ones
 To clothe
 To give to drink
 To provide
 To share
 To care

The yearning, pulling, urging from the Lord

That he has placed deep within must be satisfied

Orphans, widows, motherless, fatherless

Deliverance

My lips utter from within
I knew not this
That possessed me
My speech portray
The hidden secrets
Astonishment arose
From the depths of
My soul
I cried out for help
To Him that can
Forgive,
Purge and renew
strengthen and heal
Let my
Lips now sing
praises unto Thy name
Forever.

Enamored

The love in me
it stirs for thee
the tears that crown
my soul's entry

I marvel at
the strength of thee
How it pleased the Father
to immolate the Son

Thy love for me
does not compare
neither can measure
against mine

Thy strength and power
has enamored me
To seek and serve
for now -- throughout eternity

Faith

Faith can see
Over the highest mountain
Faith can see
To the depths of the ocean

Faith can see
Through the murky rivers
Faith can see
Through the dense forest

Faith brings clarity
In the fog –
Faith sees past the bog

Faith can see where your eyes cannot go
Faith travels through the word 'no'

Faith witnesses the impossible and calms all fears
The word of faith hears

Faith is that spiritual eye
That brings hope through the process of time

Strengths of Faith

Faith
- exists
- is matter,
- is the eyes that can see the invisible
- testifies to the existence of what is to be through time
- guides the senses and mind to the inevitable
- moves
- envelopes and procures hope
- speaks
- demonstrates
- acknowledges
- succors
- rests in God

How strong is your faith?

Grace

He shall give you more Grace
When the test seems too hard
And the trials seem too long
Just look to the hills
He will make you strong
Call on Him
He has already heard
Before you asked
It's according to His word
Trust and obey
For it's the only way
He will bring you through
With the victory, too!

He Is Everything

I am ....
   because he is my strength; my calm through the storm.

I am ...
   because he is my hope when life seems so futile.

I am ...
   because he is my love when I am longing for that special touch.

I am ...
   because he is my light when darkness comes.

I am ...
   because he is everything to me.

Oh yes, I am ...
   Because Jesus is!

His Goodness

to think of His Goodness
is most precious to me
it takes me through 'tuff times
and when I cannot see
I bask in His Glory
and in His might
for He is my strong tower
when things are not right

meditation upon Him
and upon His Word
is so inspiring and fulfilling
and though His voice be heard
barely above a whisper
I know it is Him, 'tis true
He satisfies my longing
as only He can do

so, think of His goodness
meditate upon Him
let your soul and your mind
be strengthened, Amen

Hope Eternal

Man created in God's image
Must display a holy visage

The mind of Christ formed within
Brings blessings, joy, peace to him

For those yearning to live on high
Keep your eyes pealed to the sky

He is risen for you and me
Willingly dying upon the tree

We are risen with Him, you know
Sin and shame are cast and burned below

Prayer of Confession

I cannot go it alone
    There are thoughts and feelings
    That ebb and flow as the tide
    I cannot hide these
    From thee

Lord, thou know all
    As my soul cries out
    Lord hear me

As I say unto thee
    With my thoughts and emotions
    Lord, deliver me

I cannot go it alone
    There are thoughts and feelings
    That ebb and flow as the tide
    These I cannot hide
    From thee

When I pray by faith,
    They are carried away
    And I give praises to your name

Jesus Knockin'

Jesus comes a knockin'
   At your front door

He doesn't want to be a guest
   Neither a visitor

He wants to take up abode
   Deep down within your heart

He wants to live in your soul
   And never will he depart

From you and you from him
   Won't you give Him a chance

He will bring life to you
   He'll bring a shout and a dance

He will keep His place there
   Only let Him in

Your soul will be blessed

Again and Again and Again

More Than a Conqueror

What manner of man
is this from Galilee?
Who came to set us at liberty
from our sins and woeful lives?

By his power divine
can render so much
even through a simple touch

Have we not read
the recorded word?

He is known as Jesus,
The Christ,
Wonderful Counselor,
Lord of lords,
King of kings,
Master of everything

Our finite mind goes only so far
Through him all things are possible

Don't sit there gazing
with your mouth ajar
Rejoice in him forever more
Jesus is, therefore we are

More than a conqueror

Obedience

The hills and mountains obey,
Why Can't I
The sea and the valleys bow low
Why Can't I
The rivers run deep
And praise at thy feet
Why Can't I
The fields yield their increase;
At thy Word
The trees give shade
And house the birds
They sing praise to thee in the morn
Even the new ones that are born
Why Can't I
Dry bones arose and obeyed at His command
Dry bones arose and flesh became man
It was His Word that brought life,
Life once again
To know that He "Is"
By His Power
I Can

Perfection

Too much perfection in one day
You might say,
But isn't that a command from on High?
He said to be perfect even as He is,
To be holy and righteous
Even so we must be
Just like him in character
By grace and mercy this is bestowed
Upon us
To be given a chance to experience
The heavenly
By no good works of our own
He showers us with blessings
And gifts from His endless treasure
Too much perfection in one day
You might say.

Holiness

Mere mortal words fail me
At the awesomeness of Him
To express how I feel
Is truly felt not said
To attempt the unexplainable
Is overwhelming indeed
To produce the praise
He deserves – even from the heart
Is not enough
His Holiness, His reverence
Majesty, dominion, and power
Commands love and respect

Righteous

Lord, how righteous you are
Immutable and just are your ways
You clothe us with your righteousness
And command us to live our days
Holy as you are; holy whether near or far
Not changing or zigzagging our way through
Our heart should be calling out to you
In our daily walk of life
Lord, how righteous you are
How immutable and just are your ways

Praise Your Way Thru

When you're in doubt
Can't see your way out

Praise your way thru

When you're in fear
Seems no one's near

Praise your way thru

Tho shackled by pain
In Jesus name

Praise your way thru

Does Isaiah's undoneness
Fall upon you

Praise your way thru

Don't have love for your brother?
And despise one another?

Hope is not lost
Christ paid the cost
God is in love with you!

Surrender

Oh --
> That I would surrender my heart
> The very essence of my being
> To the Savior of my soul
> My Maker, My Lord, My Keeper

Oh --
> That I would commit
> My every will, every way
> My hopes, my dreams, my aspirations

Things that I long for,
> Lord they are yours

Things that I dream about,
> Lord they are yours

My life
My love
My all --
> Lord, they are yours

The Hunter

The hunter and the hunted
    eventually will meet.

With Christ on our side
    the hunter will meet defeat
    tho' armed and dangerous
    with weapons of war.

Christ is our shield,
    Through faith we soar
    high above the hunter
    extending far out of reach

To abide in the secret place
    never to be breached
    by the hunter who seeks
    whom he may devour

Always to be defeated
By the Almighty's power!

Observe

Sit back and watch God do it
He will surely see you through it
Praising Him and worshiping Him

As he parted the Red Sea
He can surely take care of me
My sea is not wide
Where He cannot provide
My waves do not collide
Over my head, with Christ
standing in my stead

Thank you Lord for saving me
Thank you for your energy
Thank you Lord for giving to me
Everything that I need

He will supply all of my needs
He will renew my strength each day
Though I am weary
And pause by the way
I can be sure because
He is the Way!

Eternal Light

'Long as I know
'Long as I see

Your eternal light is shining down on me.

Reflections of my heart
Reflections of my soul
Eternal light is shining
Lord take control

Let your light keep shining
Eternal light keep shining down on me.

Purge out the old
Savior of my soul
Let your light keep shining down on . . .
Let your light keep shining down on . . .

As I lift my heart
As I lift my soul

Purge out the old
Savior of my soul
Let your light keep shining down on . . .
Let your light keep shining down on . . .

Let your light keep shining
Eternal light keep shining down on me.

'Long as I know
'Long as I see

Your eternal light is shining down on me.

Gates to Our Soul

Who's guarding your gates
Is Christ within

Has he dispatched guardian angels,
Set you free from sin

Has the Word taken a seat
In your life and you did eat

Till your belly was full?

Be careful what you see
Be careful what you eat
Be careful what you hear

Stay humble at His feet

He will guide you
Always beside you

Be Careful

      Some trying to go up
      the wrong way, but
      it's slippery;
      get sure footing
           Don't hesitate,
           Don't wait,
There is only a certain amount of time allowed;
Find that secret place
      Move while you have the time
           Don't wait
           Don't hesitate
Be sure,
    you're HIGH enough
    what you are holding on to is secure
Some only go so high,
Some think they're high
    but there's no strength in what they are
holding on to
Some don't move at all,
    think they have a lot of time
Some don't listen because
    they don't believe
I must tell and warn!

      BUT!!!

I must find that secret place
God will direct me; show me where to go
It's a narrow way; a pressing way -- UPWARD
    Everyone won't fit
    Some won't try
        The lion is out
        Don't hang about
God will give you strength to climb
Keep moving; don't give up
    You can be sure
    His secret place is secure.

Life

IS
...life promised or fair in it's giving

THIS
...time on earth allotted for each being, is

FOR
...a purpose, a plan to pursue, not on

SALE
...to give away as though nothing matters at all.

The Savior's Call

    "Court Me"

Am I not beautiful to you
Do I not give you what you ask of me
How comforting is my touch

    "Court Me"

When I hold you in my arms
You can feel the expression of my love
I whisper sweet peace to you

    "Court Me"

Let's meet a little early
And take a long walk together
We will communicate our deepest thoughts
Our love will have no end –

    "Court Me"

Let the Words of My Mouth

Let the words of my mouth;

> Be holy, righteous
> Pure, undefiled
> Be careful, graceful
> Kind, edify
> Speak those things that
> Be not as though they were
> Praise continually
> According to His will

Let the meditation of my heart;

> Be centered on you Lord
> Seek your will, O God
> Dwell in your love
> Commune with you in spirit
> Reflect on your Holiness

Let the fruit of my doings;

> Reflect the image of Christ
> Abound unto every good work
> Be without spot or blemish
> Be humble in thy sight

Let all be acceptable in thy sight;

> My strength
> My redeemer

A Meditation of Prayer

Lord, strengthen my mind
My will
My heart
My soul
To be thy servant O, Lord
And to do thy will
At all times ready, waiting
Listening with spiritual ears open
To God My Savior

As a true servant
Always submissive and obedient

Lord, only you alone
Can change the mind
The will
The heart
The soul
In true worship and praise
With humbleness of mind

Guided by your heavenly touch

Not to forget what you have given
As you bless straight from heaven
Good gifts all around

Good gifts that more and more abound
Bless your servant, whom you have chosen
As I meditate upon your name; your goodness
Alone can strengthen my mind
My will
My heart
My soul
To be thy servant, O, Lord
And to do thy will.

The Seed of the Woman

Born in the state of humility, lowly in a manger
Not in an earthly palace, but with animals in a stable
From a virgin, God sent His son
The omnipotent one
Lord you are able to deliver us from danger.

Lord take us thru the fire
Lord take us thru the rain
In Jesus' name.

Amen!
Jesus Christ who takes away the sins of the world
Has come to be received by many.
Those who will call upon His name to be saved
From Hell and damnation
To be united with Christ the King
From everlasting to everlasting.

Amen!
His praise is forever glorious and
is gone up before us.
To Him from those who adore and worship
Him in the beauty of holiness
Now until the end of time.

Amen!
Oh, worship Him, exalt His name
Let your mouth sing praises unto His Name
He is worthy!!

The seed of Woman who cannot sin
We will forever be with Him.
Amen!

Black and White

The colors of black and white
Truly has started many a fight
Why do we stop at the surface of skin?
When truly we know its sin
That which lies within the man
Provokes him to do all he can
Against mankind and every other
That God only intended to be his brother
It doesn't matter your outside look
But you can be transformed by the Book
Ready and willing to do His will
If only we can stand still,
Get involved with the Master's Plan
Then we can truly say that "I AM"
Has granted me to give up the fight
Of the colors with black and white.

A Pebble

...one small stone, not very heavy
lays on the beach soaking up the sun.

Too small to trip over, not big enough to bruise the toe,

But with one giant hand God causes this pebble to be

Thrown out into the water, in the deep
To appear as though never to be found again,

But where this one small pebble lands does not

Necessarily make a big splash, but causes the water to move which creates action and motion visible to the eye

But this one small pebble may never be seen again; but will forever be remembered -- for the movement.

Be what God called you to be –
If you are a pebble, be not afraid to
Get thrown into the water to cause much action

Be the One

To touch somebody's heart
To light somebody's way

The salt of the earth

To season with joy
        preserve in hope
        sustain in righteousness
        embrace in love

Desperately Aware

Are we desperately aware
of the depth of our need?
Blind men can't see, lame men can't walk,
there are the maimed; those who cannot talk
The poor are desperately aware

The starving
know the depth of their despair
Have we ears to hear,
do we see with our eyes,
can we walk

What is the depth
Who will make us aware?

Our sin sick soul
Cries out for the living God

Oh – to know the depth
to be aware
To desperately cry
from the depths
To long for him who can supply
even through our despair

To reach the depth
unknown in the natural
yet, into the spiritual
To be made aware

Of the desperation of the depth
Of our despair

Is our Savior and Lord
Desperately Aware

Are we desperately aware
of the depth of our need?
Blind men can't see, lame men can't walk,
there are the maimed; those who cannot talk
The poor are desperately aware

The starving
know the depth of their despair
Have we ears to hear,
do we see with our eyes,
can we walk

What is the depth
Who will make us aware?

Our sin sick soul
Cries out for the living God

Oh – to know the depth
to be aware
To desperately cry
from the depths
To long for him who can supply
even through our despair

To reach the depth
unknown in the natural
yet, into the spiritual
To be made aware

Of the desperation of the depth
Of our despair

Is our Savior and Lord

In the Process of Time

Deliverance will come
Saith the Lord
In the process of time
Healing will come
In the process of time
Saith, the Lord of Hosts

Trust in Him
There's healing in His wings
Trust in Him
For all things
Surely it is in His hands
Lord God Almighty
The Sovereign One!

Thank you, Lord
For the morning light
Thank you for keeping me through the night
With your glory and your hope
I can face the day

Is it hard?

When life seems to get you down
Remember to turn that frown around
It's only a test.
When you press your way
And look for a brighter day
God is with you
While you are yet going through
It's only a test.
Sometimes tests are hard
And we get stumped
Remember – it's only a test
Test were not made to break us
But bring us through and make us
Test were not made
To see what you don't know
But what you do
So remember the end – it's coming soon
God has not forgotten you
It's only a test.
There is a reward in the end
The press is to send it to you
So – when it seems that life has gotten you down
Turn that frown around
It's only a test.
When it seems all hope is lost
God has counted up the cost

In tears and prayers
And righteousness too
He has not forgotten you
Though the test be long and dreary
You seem to get weary
Wait upon the Lord
It is in His word
He will renew your strength

Love Announces Itself

Greater love hath no man
As the Bible say
God announces the coming of his son
For God so loved the world that he gave
Who do we so love?
Are we giving?
Does our love announce itself?
Let my love speak to my brother
Who I see everyday
Let my love be spread abroad
My compassion demonstrated in a holy way
My love should represent the love of Christ
Who I see by faith.

Life

Is but a vapor
Eternity is (forever) everlasting
Vapor is a mist moving,
shifting into the unknown

Your Presence,

...captivates my senses
as your spirit fills the room.

I embrace the sweetness,
that gently caresses the strings of my heart.

Filling my soul with such love, and spilling over
from the depths of my inner being.

I become overwhelmed and refreshed by my
living waters to experience life everlasting from
this moment on...

Women of Excellence

In prayer, worship and acknowledgement
To our Father in Heaven
Glory to His name, forever

He has bestowed upon us wisdom
To be prudent befitting our character

He has gathered us together
With complete diligence in holy stewardship

As we exemplify temperate behavior,
There is balance in our natural
There is balance in our spiritual

We speak life, health and healing
To our mind, body and spirit

There is integrity in our walk, as well as our talk

Power from the most High enables us to
Sow -
Grow -
Change -
As ambassadors, In Jesus' name

We have more disciples to win
With excellent motion, in complete and humble devotion

By faith and in unity
We celebrate a full harvest

We are our Sister's Keeper!

PLEA

Children on our streets
    - with guns –
experiencing the heat
they should have never known,
the burning of the flesh,
the stench of the night,
How could this be?

Children abandoned by father, then mother
Left to raise themselves,
    - only -
they don't know nothin' bout raisin'
growing up or maturing.
The mother, the father are held accountable
To God,
not the children for their raisin'.

Where did the anger come from against one another?
Always fussing, fighting and killing their brother;
love could have been there
if they had their mother
to nurture and tend to the needs of her children.

Fathers, don't breed out as many as you can.
Stand up, be accountable, be that man
who can help their son to know right from wrong.

Teach them how to pray, grow up, be strong,
physically, spiritually and mentally tough
so they can be accountable to their sons
and pass on wisdom and knowledge with
the strength to be strong.

The Flower of Life...

...it blooms but for a moment,
To open up in His Glory -- to our God.
To perfume the air with expressions of Praise

To soak in His rain of blessings
To grow in His fullness
To take root and have life in His soil
Drenched, saturated in riches

Ahhhh - but as the flower,
Our life is just for a moment.
As we fold up in humble submission
Surrendering to His will.

"My Prayer"

That I may acknowledge your presence
And my concern is towards your view of me.

For in your view there is truth, love and mercy
Your understanding surpasses,
Yea - cannot compare to that of man
Your ways are past finding out!

That my concern is towards your view of me
For in that I find deliverance; there is healing
and comfort, too.

You see what is there, and
Your light reveals the truth.

Who can know the heart of man, but God?
Who dares to compare himself to the most High?
Yea – we are exposed.

In your truth there is love for our sinful
condition to bring to deliverance that which man
cannot do.

In your love there is mercy and unmerited favor
To forgive –

By your mercy, we are forgiven.

That I may acknowledge your presence
And my concern is towards your view of me.

That I may praise and glorify your name –
forever!
Amen.

On One Note:
The Horrors of Society

Can you answer the question, why?

Why are there horrors of society
     in the land of the free, the home of the
     brave?

 Why do we live in fear of our neighbor who we
      thought
   was our friend

Can you answer the question, why?
     Why is the public protector who should
     be my friend has now,
     become my abuser, enemy, someone
     to suspect, not trust.

The badge was safety --
     Safety has failed

The badge was comfort--
     Comfort is gone

The badge was security--
   The homeland is laid bare and open
   No safety, no comfort, no security at home

Can you answer the question why?
   In the land of the free, the home of the brave?

My Enemy

Let's embrace each other in love
Peace and harmony

You're not my enemy
 God loves you and I do too
We belong to him
We are forever His people

Let's embrace each other in love
Peace and harmony

Of course, there were times
When we did not agree,
When we couldn't see,
When we didn't hear,
Of course, there were times,

But God gives us the victory

Let's embrace each other in love
Peace and harmony
You're not my enemy

Through God's only begotten Son
We have the victory

The Awesomeness of God

Just like the ocean cannot be comprehended
The awesomeness of God
Just like the ocean

I knew you Jeremiah before you were known
The awesomeness of God
Just like the ocean

The depths of the seas Who can know it
The awesomeness of God
Just like the ocean

Number of hairs on my head
Just like the ocean

How far can you see? Let faith carry you.

I place my right foot at the edge of the ocean
and then place my left foot alongside of it.
I become overwhelmed by the strength and the
sight of it which engulfs me and
I am become lost within the swirls and
movements along the shoreline.

How vast and incomprehensible is the

    Width – Breadth – Height

Who can know it, but God?
I am brought in tune with reality size,
the significance of stance,
the strength of voice space.

His glory cannot be exposed within the confines
of the mind although I press to understand.
What is my request that I should be allowed to
present it before His glory?

How can I even begin to understand what is
already done?
What is yet to come, becoming in Him. I cannot.

But yet, I praise Him because He is.
He has accepted me as his friend
I embrace His love, grace and mercy within
my mind -- my bosom
Yes, my soul.

Women of God

Which are rare indeed
Giving ourselves
To feed the lost soul who hungers
And thirst for a savior
We as servants humbly meet the need

Now is not the time to fold up in fear
We are precious in the eyesight of God
Gems, rich, red and dark like rubies
Highly valued, delicate and strong.
Our quality surpasses the emerald and diamond
The ruby rare who can find one.

My price just went up!

www.ingramcontent.com/pod-product-compliance
Lightning Source LLC
LaVergne TN
LVHW051511070426
835507LV00022B/3056